To Sade :

Thank You
For Checking In ? On Me!

May God Continue To
Bless You!

Please Know He Loves You
& So Do I.

Mom (Star)
Sharlette

WHY STORMS

ARE NEEDED

3 Stages of Faith

WRITTEN BY:

SHARLETTE M. FRANKLIN

.

WHY STORMS

ARE NEEDED

3 Stages of Faith

WRITTEN BY:

SHARLETTE M. FRANKLIN

Copyright 2/2005   All rights reserved

ISBN: 978-0-6151-7669-7

Table of Contents

Table of Contents Cont'd

~ Forward~

First, giving thanks to my Heavenly Father, my Big Brother and Savior, Jesus, and my Comforter and Reminder of the word, Holy Spirit, for guiding me in the midst of pain to rise up for such a time as this.

I have been blessed so many times while writing this book, and reminded to get up and not be beaten down by the storms of my life.

I can truly say, that God will use your own words at a later date to remind you of His greatness.

God has healed me through this book in many areas of my faith and now I release it to be a blessing.

~ *Honor to My Spiritual Mentors*~

Aside from God, my Pastor, Bishop Kenneth C. Ulmer, Juanita Bynum and the late Kenneth Hagin Sr. were the teachers that stuck to my heart.

Without even their knowledge, they compelled me to endure hardness as a good soldier and to never give up!

Bishop Ulmer, thank you for teaching me how to live in today's society in victory. Thank you for teaching me the three dimensional revelations of God's truth.

You are a great man of integrity that has always shown the transparency of his heart and revealed your own shortcomings. This helps us to know that we are not alone and honor God for sending you to us.

You have no idea how much you mean to me and how I believe that God has connected us in the spirit. I admire you and hold you in the highest regard.

You are my spiritual FATHER who encourages me to be the woman of integrity without compromise.

It is my honor to travel 100 miles every week to be on my post at church and minister in the pews as you minister on the pulpit.

I want you to be proud of me as your spiritual daughter. As part of the Road Team, I enjoy going out with you to other events. I love and pray for you and your family daily.

As I go out to minister, I proudly carry the mantle of my spiritual, intellectual, brilliant and loving hearted father with me.

Bishop, thank you just seems so inadequate.

I thank God for Juanita Bynum for displaying my life through her own as if I were looking in a mirror. I can see myself like her Mini-Me.

She encourages me to pursue excellence and not take down to anything or anyone that says a woman is limited.

Finally, and most early in my life, was the late great Rev. Kenneth Hagin Sr. who taught me about the concept of faith.

He taught me through his books how to love God by faith. I learned that everything I would come to know about God, I would have to use my faith to bring it to pass!

~ *Dedications* ~
(In Glory Land)

In loving memory of my mom, Mattie Frances Parks, who allowed me to care for her in the midst of her storm of small-cell cancer.

I thank God for such a woman of Grace and Elegance.

She taught me how love God through embracing others and loving them unconditionally. She was the example of the neighborhood mother that everyone wanted to be around.

I know that she lives on in me as I continue to reach out to the least.

~~~~~~~~~~~~~~~~~~~~~~~~~~~~~~~~~~

~~~~~~~~~~~~~~~~~~~~~~~~~~~~~

In memory of my sister and prayer partner Norma, who was instrumental in helping me start a women's prayer ministry called Women of Valor. We met every Friday morning for intercessory prayer at 5:00 am.

Her passion and concern for our nation and the people lost in the world without God made her a radical blessing to the Kingdom of God. She will always be with me.

Finally, in memory of my eldest sister Sha'Ron, that suddenly left us without warning; thank you for sharing your faith and humor. I see you always in the mirror. I look just like you. You too are always with me.

(In the land of the living)

To my beloved sons:

Lester and Shawntelle, thank you for giving me the courage and the motivation to wake up everyday and keep trying. Everything I have done has been for you. God knew that giving you to me was the key to keeping me alive.

Thank you for loving me in spite of my many mistakes! You are the reason that I know God loves me!

What an honor to be your mom!

To my mija, Ivette:

What can I say? I love you and I appreciate you for all that you do and bring to my life. You have been a great disciple and yet a daughter that only God could have put in my life.

Thank you for your tireless efforts of proofing and giving me encouragement. You are my Mini Me!

To my Daddy,

Rev. Shearwood Fleming Sr., your nuggets of wisdom have always spoken to me in the time of need. Just know that I do value everything that you have taught me. Thank you for loving me. I am your chocolate child.

To my brother Shearwood Jr., thanks for being my inspiration. There is no one that I know who has endured more than you. I find strength from watching you deal with the storms of your life. I love you.

To my sister Sheila, what an incredible woman you have come to be. I thank God for the lessons you have taught me. Without you, I would not be as strong in prayer. I pray for you daily.

Thank you for stepping in and being the mom for Special and Ukari. God loves you and so do I, no matter what comes. Bless you.

To my brother Steven, I love you. There is a time for you to shine and bring out what God has put inside of you. Be encouraged and know that God has not forgotten you.

*Keep the honor of our parents before
you as your guide.*

*To the many other thousands of
children across the country that God
has given to me spiritually, I love you
and find great joy in sitting around
the fireplace or chatting at the coffee
shop about how great our God is.*

*You have brought great purpose and
passion to my life like I never knew
possible. I look forward to many
more moments.*

*To my family that remains, it is my
prayer that we never lose sight of
God.*

*We have been through so much and I
love you all.*

Finally, thanks to you, the reader for opening the pages of this book.

I wanted to share with you a word that God has spoken to me in the midst of going through several storms in my life and finding answers as to why I had to go through them.

It is my will to be an obedient vessel unto God. I want love to abide in you as you witness God's love towards you and others, even the world.

My prayer for you is that this book serves as a helpful tool to understand why you are going through storms and what exactly is happening in your lives.

I have discovered that none of us are exempt from pain or tragedy. I have also discovered that in the midst of it, we are not alone.

I couldn't have been alone, because my legs didn't have the strength to stand on their own.

Someone had to be holding me up. Only God could hold me up after all that I have been through.

God has shared with me life-changing revelation regarding the storms of our lives and how we are to handle them and ourselves.

He gives us keys to our victory in the midst of our storm.

Be encouraged and know that you are not alone; no matter how alone you may feel.

Again, thank you for taking time to receive this blessing from our Heavenly Father. He loves you!

JN 3:16 For **God so loved the world**, that he gave his only begotten Son, that whosoever believeth in him should not perish, but have everlasting life.

~ Chapter 1 ~

<u>Questions & Clarifications</u>

Have you ever thought about the reason storms come?

Have you ever stood outside in the midst of a storm and looked up?

Has there ever been a time when the storm came and all you could do was look outside from a window, feeling like you couldn't move because the storm was so bad?

Did you answer yes to those questions?

Well let us explore this next question and answer it to the best of your ability and with all honesty.

1. Why are storms needed?

This is the question that most people have asked at one time or another in their lives.

Yet when asking all of these questions, we're really not trying to find the answers. We just want relief from the storm so that we can continue to do what we want to do.

God has a reason for all things, including the storms.

He alone knows the necessity of what storms would bring and then imparts that wisdom to us (mankind).

As we go on this journey of discovery together, truth will be revealed to us as to why it IS necessary for us to endure the storms of our lives.

Let's look at the question "Why are storms needed?" from the biblical perspective.

There are at least three reasons for the necessity of storms that God has revealed to me.

I was so blessed by what God showed me that I wanted to share it with you.

Storms come in our lives to help us develop our faith. There is a 3-step process. This process is as follows:

1. To Discover your faith
2. To Challenge your faith
3. To Increase your faith

According to the scriptures found in Luke 8:22-25, Jesus speaks to the winds and the waves (storms) and they obey him.

This was an amazing miracle that challenged and tested the faith of the disciples.

The passages read like this:

LK 8:22 Now it came to pass on one of those days, that he entered into a boat, himself and his disciples; and he said unto them, Let us go over unto the other side of the lake: and they launched forth.

LK 8:23 But as they sailed he fell asleep: and there came down a storm of wind on the lake; and they were filling `with water', and were in jeopardy.

LK 8:24 And they came to him, and awoke him, saying, Master, master, we perish. And he awoke, and rebuked the wind and the raging of the water: and they ceased, and there was a calm.

LK 8:25 And he said unto them, Where is your faith? And being afraid they marveled, saying one to another, Who then is this, that he commandeth even the winds and the water, and they obey him?

In verse 22 it says that on a certain day, Jesus went into a ship with the disciples.

That lets us know that God knows the very moment when we will go through a test.

It means that there is an appointed time for you and me to experience whatever God has for us to go through.

In that same verse it also says that Jesus went into the ship with the disciples.

He assures us that the feeling of loneliness is not necessary and confirms that we are NEVER alone.

Even though there are times when it seems like we are going through the worst of things by ourselves, Jesus tells us that He will never leave us nor forsake us.

HEB 13:5 *Let your conversation be without covetousness; and be content with such things as ye have: for he hath said,* **I will never leave thee, nor forsake thee.**

Jesus says to the disciples "Let us go over to the other side". In this moment we see that Jesus is not a mute.

"Let us go over unto the other side of the lake"

Jesus speaks to us!

He gives us comfort and assurance of who He is by speaking victory of our journey to us, even in the beginning of our experience.

There are two scriptures that give me comfort as a witness to our victory in Jesus.

*1COR 15:57 But thanks be to God, which giveth us the **victory** through our Lord Jesus Christ.*

*1JN 5:4 For whatsoever is born of God overcometh the world: and this is the **victory** that overcometh the world, even **our faith**.*

Think about a time when you were not sure of the outcome of your situation and God spoke to you about a clear victory.

God shares His word that we are overcomers if we are born again. We have already won the victory!

We know going in that we have already won and we just have to go through the process.

God loves us so much that He made sure that we knew that if He were for us, that He was more than the world against us.

ROM 8:31 What shall we then say to these things? **If God be for us**, who can be against us?

It's important that in the face of the storm, we must remember that God has given us a 3-step process for our faith to develop and become strong.

~ *Chapter 2* ~

<u>*Hearing the Voice of God*</u>

Despite what others may think when they say that they can't hear from God, just know that it is NOT because He is not speaking.

I used to think that He couldn't hear me when I cried out to Him. And believe me, I cried loud!

But then one day after going through what I thought was one of the worst moments of my life, God spoke to me and told me that I would make it!

I was stricken with hemiplegic migraines caused by too much stress and the disease to please.

As a result of taking care of everyone else and neglecting myself, the migraines became increasingly worse and lead to the unthinkable.

*I suffered a **STROKE, BLINDNESS and COMPLETE PARALYSIS ON MY LEFT SIDE!***

I needed a miracle and I needed it right then. I needed to know that the God of my salvation was able to speak to me and assure me of His presence.

God did exactly that and told me to be a good steward of my situation.

He told me that He was going to get glory out of the situation even though the doctor told me that I was going to die!

God told me that this illness would not be unto death, but that through it He was going to strengthen my witness for Him.

*While taking over 12 different medications, I **seemed** to be getting worse.*

I became allergic to several of the medications, as the combination of a few was counteractive.

I asked God to get me through it and help me to be a good steward of this storm.

God allowed me to know that He was with me in several ways, but the most loving way that He spoke to me was with a touch. His touch!

I'm reminded of the scripture of the woman with the issue of blood that pushed through the crowd, in spite of her "unclean" disposition, she said, "if I can touch the hem of His garment, I'll be made whole"

God gave me His touch in the sweetest manner.

I had a couch that sat against a wall under a picture window.

Since there was no feeling on my left side, I had to sleep where God would wake me up every morning by sunlight.

Because of the blindness, when I opened my eyes the only thing I could see was darkness.

The only way I knew that morning had come, was when God would kiss me on my right cheek with the warmth of sunlight.

This was God saying to me, "It's not over yet, and I have more for you to do".

I became more determined to fight the fight of faith and let God be glorified.

I took the medicines that were making me sicker and threw them away!

I'm not saying that anyone should ever do that if your faith is not at that level, but I believed God and I wanted Him to heal me.

Within two months, my eyesight was returned and the paralysis was wearing off.

I was scheduled to speak at a women's conference within a month of that time and by the time of the conference, I was there and spoke the entire three days!

This is a testimony of God's great healing and blessings in my life. God showed himself to be Jehovah Rapha, the Lord that heals.

I know that God speaks and I am learning to listen to His voice.

Sometimes I have been so busy and in such a hurry, that I missed God's voice and paid the consequences of not being still long enough to hear His instructions.

He speaks the ending in the beginning, and then backs up and walks with us "through" its completion.

He does this over and over again with us through each storm that we encounter.

But He does it "with" us.
We are NEVER alone!

Back to the scripture of Luke 8:22 where Jesus says "let us", which means it is inclusive of Him being with us and not sending us into the storm alone.

He says, "Let us go over". Go meaning action as opposed to being stagnant. We are to be active in God's kingdom.

Jesus understood the lesson He was about to teach the disciples.

After all, He knew that His whole purpose of spending time with the disciples.

Jesus was teaching and preparing them for the time when He wouldn't be there physically, but they were to still keep their faith in tact.

Lesson 1:

** DISCOVERY **

This lesson was to prepare them to be "storm watchers" and yet be able to speak to the storms themselves.

They would speak with the power and faith that Jesus would impart to them.

All this was being taught in this one journey.

So, Jesus continues to say, "let us go over".

The word "Over" here in Greek is pleonazo meaning "to abound or super abound".

So it says, let us together take action to abound or super abound to the other side. Let's go beyond this point and onto the other side.

The bible says that after Jesus spoke to them; they obeyed and launched out on the journey.

The greatest way to form deep relationship with God is to be "obedient".

When we listen to the voice of God rather than our own senses, we move beyond our limitations and find hope in God.

*Our strength is renewed and faith is **<u>DISCOVERED</u>**.*

Lesson 2:

** CHALLENGE **

In verse 23 of Luke chapter 8, a CHALLENGE came to the disciples' faith when the storm of **wind** fell upon the water and began to fill the ship.

They were afraid and went to Jesus who was asleep and begged Him to save them.

There will be times in our lives when we are challenged in a particular area.

Follow the steps of the disciples and cry out to Jesus and ask Him to save you!

*Many people have focused on the fact that the disciples **lost** their faith, but I beg to differ.*

They still had enough faith within them to cry out to Jesus for him to make the storm cease.

Their faith was <u>challenged</u> by the overwhelming storm that they saw with their physical eyes and it was then that they panicked.

LK 8:24 And they came to him, and awoke him, saying, Master, master, we perish.

This scripture shows their true humanity and their need for God to assure them that He was with them.

God wouldn't fail them when they needed to be saved.

God loves us so much that He will deliver us out of our trouble, even when our faith isn't at its greatest.

Lesson 3:

** INCREASE **

*The disciples' faith **INCREASED** the very moment Jesus spoke to the storm and it ceased.*

They were in awe of Jesus and yet, at the same time, the fear of the Lord and the reverence of the Lord became a reality.

They knew in whom they had their faith especially after seeing such an awesome miracle.

Finally, in verse 25 Jesus looked at His disciples and asked them the question that would cause them to start their process all over again.

Jesus asked them "Where is your faith?"

The bible says that the disciples were afraid and marveled at what had just taken place when the winds and waves obeyed Jesus' command and were stilled.

They couldn't even respond to Jesus, but they did whisper amongst themselves "What manner of man is this that the winds and waves obey His command?"

Right then and there all three levels of faith occurred almost simultaneously.

*Their faith was (1) re- **discovered** when Jesus recognized their faith as ALWAYS being existent. He was asking them to pull it out of hiding, because it did exist.*

*Jesus (2) **challenged** their faith, based on the fact that this was NOT the first miracle that the disciples had witnessed.*

Jesus hoped that by now they would have used the faith that was in them to speak things into existence just as He did.

As followers of Jesus, they were in a classroom 24 hours a day/7days a week. In other words "At all times".

Always learning lessons about the right thing to do and/or say.

*As Jesus caused them to **discover** and **challenge** their faith, they believed that He was the Son of the Living God.*

*Lastly, their faith was (3) **increased** to the point that there was nothing else to say after experiencing that moment with Jesus.*

We've all been in situations where Jesus caused us to look deep within ourselves and discover our faith.

It seems like it's by accident, but it was already orchestrated by God.

Because we have a free will, it is a good thing that we can know with confidence that there is someone that we can all call on when our will fails.

As God speaks to us, make sure that your ear is inclined to hear His voice.

~ *Chapter 3* ~

<u>*Natural vs. Spiritual*</u>

Everything God says to us has a natural and a spiritual meaning. Jesus spoke and taught through many parables.

Parables are natural stories that have an underlying spiritual meaning.

There are many parables that Jesus spoke to his disciples in the company of various groups of people.

Paul spoke to the Ephesians' Church in terms of being soldiers and making sure that they were properly dressed with their amour.

This was practical terminology they clearly understood.

EPH 6:11 **Put on the whole armour of God,** *that ye may be able to stand against the wiles of the devil.*

EPH 6:12 For we wrestle not against flesh and blood, but against principalities, against powers, against the rulers of the darkness of this world, against spiritual wickedness in high places.

EPH 6:13 Wherefore take unto you the whole armour of God, that ye may be able to withstand in the evil day, and having done all, to stand.

EPH 6:14 Stand therefore, having your loins girt about with truth, and having on the breastplate of righteousness;

EPH 6:15 And your feet shod with the preparation of the gospel of peace;

EPH 6:16 Above all, taking the shield of faith, wherewith ye shall be able to quench all the fiery darts of the wicked.
EPH 6:17 And take the helmet of salvation, and the sword of the Spirit, which is the word of God:

Unless we have an understanding of our uniform, we will not utilize it properly.

You can't wear you shoes on your hands or your helmet on your feet.

Every piece of armour has a specific purpose and protection attached to it!

God knew that and that's why He gives it to us in the order He does.

*When I speak God's word over me, by putting on His armour before I get out of bed each morning, I can almost feel it coming upon me.
It is awesome!*

For when God tells us to put on the whole armour of God, He clearly gives us the spiritual aspect in His word.

By pointing out the natural pieces of outer armour, God then reveals to us its spiritual meaning and importance.

God wants for us as Christians, to present ourselves in such a way that men, would not be shocked or appalled at our presentation of Christ in our lives!

God requires us to be fit for the battle!

~ *Chapter 4* ~

<u>*What type of storm is it?*</u>

Our battle can be described as a storm.

We can think of storms in several ways.

Webster's dictionary defines it as follows:

[1]*storm*

Pronunciation: `'storm`
Function: noun
1 a : *a disturbance of the atmosphere marked by wind and usually by rain, snow, hail, sleet, or thunder and*

There are several types of storms.

Let me give you several examples and their meaning.

[1]*rain*

Pronunciation: `'rAn`
Function: noun
1 a : *water falling in drops condensed from vapor in the atmosphere*

[1]*hur·ri·cane*

Pronunciation: `'hur-i-"kAn, -i-kAn, 'hu-ri-, 'hu-ri-`
Function: noun
1 : *a tropical cyclone with winds of 74 miles (118 kilometers) per hour or greater that occurs especially in the western Atlantic, that is usually accompanied by rain, thunder, and lightning, and that sometimes moves into temperate latitudes*

[1]*hail*

Pronunciation: `'hA(&)l`
Function: noun
1 : *precipitation in the form of small balls or lumps usually consisting of concentric layers of clear ice and compact snow*

¹*snow*

Pronunciation: `'snO`
Function: noun
1 a : *precipitation in the form of small white ice crystals formed directly from the water vapor of the air at a temperature of less than 32°F (0°C*

¹*wind*

Pronunciation: `'wind, archaic or poetic 'wInd`
Function: noun
1 a : *a natural movement of air of any velocity; especially : the earth's air or the gas surrounding a planet in natural motion horizontally*

thun·der·storm

Pronunciation: `-"storm`
Function: noun
: *a storm accompanied by lightning and thunder*

¹*thun·der*

Pronunciation: `'thun-der`
Function: noun
1 : the sound that follows a flash of lightning and is caused by sudden expansion of the air in the path of the electrical discharge
2 : a loud utterance or threat

tor·na·do

Pronunciation: `tor-'nA-(")dO`
Function: noun
1 archaic : a tropical thunderstorm
2 a : a squall accompanying a thunderstorm in Africa b : a violent destructive whirling wind accompanied by a funnel-shaped cloud that progresses in a narrow path over the

No matter what storm comes your way, you need to know that trouble does not always last.

Here are some benefits after the storm.

The air is cleanest immediately right after a storm.

*In order for some things to be cleaned up in our lives, God must send the storm of **His choice**.*

Sometimes we get so caught up in things that look like they are good for us and then, before we know it, we are in a mess with something bigger than we can handle!

That's when those famous words begin to proceed from our mouths, saying, "Lord, if you just get me out of this mess, I'll serve you"!

Or if you don't' have that much time, the words "Lord help!" always are available!

God in His infinite wisdom then answers our cry and cleans up our mess with a storm.

Being in the storm may sometimes be uncomfortable. Because you may get a little wet or windblown, you must understand that the sun is soon to follow and will dry up what needs to be dried.

The area in your life that appeared to be dead simply needed to be resurrected. God used the rain to bring new life.

So thank God for the storms.

Don't complain!

Know that even though it may seem tough, God is still in control and knows what's best for you.

God wants for you to have life and that more abundantly.

*JN 10:10 The thief cometh not, but for to steal, and to kill, and to destroy: I am come that they might have life, and that they might have it more **abundantly**.*

*There has to be a **balance**.*

He does not want you to be in the sun at all times.

For there, your life would soon become a desert.

Everything would eventually dry up, wither and die.

You must have a storm in your life every now and then to keep the moisture in the air whenever it is needed.

In order for you to enjoy the fruit of the land (both physically and spiritually) there must be fertile ground.

The soil must be soaked with the water from God in order to produce life.

Give thanks for the rain and know that the rain represents the blessings of God coming fourth.

So let the storms come, the harder the storm is to bear, the greater is the blessing that follows.

~ *Chapter 5* ~

Keep Praise on Your Lips

David, said in Psalms:

I will Bless the Lord at all times and His praise shall continually be in my mouth!

*PS 34:1 **I will bless the LORD at all times**: his praise shall continually be in my mouth.*

He goes on to say:

My soul shall make her boast in the Lord, the humble shall hear thereof and be glad

PS 34:2 My soul shall make her boast in the LORD: the humble shall hear thereof, and be glad.

So my brother and my sister, I want you to know that we must bless the Lord in the midst of the storm.

Know that the dirty areas of your life are being washed whiter than snow by the mighty hand of God.

In the 34th chapter of Psalms, David references our tastes buds toward the Lord.

PS 34:8 O taste and see that the LORD is good: blessed is the man that trusteth in him.

Trusting in God and what He is doing in our lives will put a song or two in our hearts.

It is important that you keep a song in your heart.

I'm reminded of an old song that the elders used to sing that simply says: I'm so glad, that troubles don't last always.

Another song says:
The storm is passing over.

*The truth is just that, the storm **is** passing over!*

We must take comfort in knowing that nothing lasts forever, not even the storm we may be facing right now.

Jesus said to His disciples "in this life you will suffer persecution", but to be of good cheer, for He had already, overcome the world.

*JN 16:33 These things I have spoken unto you, that in me ye might have peace. In the world ye shall have tribulation: but be of good cheer; **I have overcome the world***

Just the mere fact that Jesus said He had already overcome the world, even before we suffered the persecution, is such an awesome thing to conceive.

Before we go through the hard or challenging situations, God has already given us the victory.

It is now our job to face the storm knowing that the umbrella of God and all of the heavenly hosts covers us.

~ *Chapter 6* ~

<u>Graduation Day!</u>

As a matter of fact, when the storms come, we must begin to rejoice!

Rejoice? You might say what are you talking about? Rejoice, but How? I say yes! Rejoice!

Because that means that you have graduated!

You have graduated from one blessing and are being ushered into your next victory with showers of blessings to accompany you.

So, Rejoice!
I don't know how God is going to bless you, but now is the time to get ready for that blessing.

As we go through the storms, let us embrace them and see what purpose they serve.

Whether the storm is from the rain that washes away the dirt and cleanses us...

Or snow that freezes the cancerous elements that try to kill us....

Maybe it's the windstorm that blows away the impurities and clears the smog...

God uses the storms to carry away the things that are too heavy on us.

Whether it is thunder that reminds us of the bolstering problems...

We must know that God knows why the storms are needed

And now...so do we!

Through every type of storm, our Faith is discovered, challenged and increased.

The bible declares in Hebrews 11:6, that without faith, it is IMPOSSIBLE to please God.

[6] But without faith it is impossible to please him: for he that cometh to God must believe that he is, and that he is a rewarder of them that diligently seek him.

Whatever faith you have, use it to the glory of God and you will see that you can measure where you are in the various stages of your storm.

*If you are trying to figure it out, then you are in **discovery**.*

*If you are in the overwhelming stage, then you are in **challenge** mode.*

*And finally, if the storm has been calmed, then you are now in the **increased** stage of your faith and you are ready to face the next storm. However, don't think that the same type of storm is coming your way.*

Just know that the <u>stages of each</u> type of storm are the same.

In terms of developing your faith, each type of storm will be a stepping-stone.

*These stepping-stones serve to **discover**, **challenge** or test, and finally **increase** your faith.*

This faith that you are developing is not just for you!

It is also for you to NOW be a helper to someone else going through a storm that you have already had victory over.

YOU will become the vessel of God to be used to increase your brother or sister in Christ.

Amen!

Because of coming through your storms, you now will discover purpose in your life!

Now it is time for you to share your testimony of how God has brought you through the storm.

God is to receive ALL the Glory!

You have to remember that you were not in that storm alone and you can receive no credit for calming the storm.

It was the faith you had in God to bring you through, which caused every storm in your past to pass.

It is the faith in God you now possess that will keep you peaceful, sane and steadfast in the midst of a storm.

As your faith grows, it will serve as the motivation you will need to journey successfully through your next storm.

Congratulations on graduating to your next victory.

You already have the tools necessary to succeed through the next victory.

Know that you are on a constant journey of beginning and ending.

Don't be caught off guard and don't blame the enemy.

As long as you have your armour on, you will defeat the enemy.

Your storm will not overtake you, but just as Jesus spoke to the winds and waves, you too will need to speak to that storm and it too will obey.

God has blessed you to be able to handle this storm and the next one that will come.

I said there is another storm on the way!

Don't be afraid. Be prepared!

The great victory for you is in KNOWING that you can journey through to the other side as a champion!

~ *Chapter 7* ~

Testify

Now, there is YOUR story that has to be told. God has brought you through something in this life and it must be told.

Whether you think it to be small or insignificant, you do have a story.

That story must be shared with someone and it WILL encourage them.

Your life is a testimony!

Testify to someone else of your victory and how you made it through the storm.

You must understand that there is something <u>greater</u> than even going through the storm.

As I mentioned earlier, you must focus on helping someone else through their storm by sharing your faith in God and how He has helped you over to the other side.

You know that there are serious issues that you have brought before the Lord in prayer.

These are some of the most private things that you haven't even discussed with your closest friend.

You know that if you were to share these issues with someone other than God, you would probably be misunderstood.

Give God your best and His best will ALWAYS be yours!

Go and testify to someone else of God's goodness towards you and be a blessing to their lives.

God brought me through the stroke, blindness and paralysis.

Later He brought me through the storm of losing my mom and two sisters all within 18 months!

He even gave me strength to preach one of their eulogies and sing at the others' funeral.

Since that was the most recent of storms, I am trusting God to do great and supernatural things in the aftermath of these storms.

When you think you can't go any further and that you are about to give up, God will send a refreshing cool wind to blow upon you.

To this day, when I get discouraged, I can still feel God's warm sunlight kiss on my right cheek, which encourages me to go on.

~ *Why are storms needed?* ~

To develop our faith
(Discover, Challenge & Increase)

***To fulfill God's Word**

PS 148:8 Fire, and hail; snow, and vapors;
***stormy** wind fulfilling his word:*

***To show forth God's power**

*NAHUM 1:3 The LORD is slow to anger, and
great in power, and will not at all acquit the
wicked: the LORD hath his way in the
whirlwind and in the **storm**, and the clouds are
the dust of his feet.*

*God bless you as you victoriously go
through your storm!*

***Look for these next two books coming soon.**

Now bless God you as you victoriously go through your storm!

Sing a song of worship and lift your hands in total surrender to God.

For God is great and worthy to be praised.

Here are a couple of worship songs that God gave me in the midst of my storms and you can trust God to give you a song in the midst of your storm as well.

Psalms 33:says to "Sing unto Him a new song!"

Sing Zion, Sing!

Lord, I surrender to You...Me

Written By Sharlette M. Franklin
11/3/05 during a fast of direction

Father, I stretch my hand to Thee

Please hear my earnest plea
I need your availability

For this is my reality
Lord I know,
I need to surrender to you....Me

Chorus

So here I am Lord
Kneeling at your throne
Realizing Lord
That I can't do this on my own

I need your help Lord
I can't survive Lord
I need to confess Lord
I need to surrender to you,.... Me

If you can calm the raging sea
and speak peace to the wind

You can mend my broken heart
And come live within

You open blinded eyes to see
and caused the lame to walk

Now I'm asking You
To forgive me Lord
For all my iniquity

Lord, I surrender to You….Me

Have your way Lord
May your will be done in my life

Guide my footsteps
That I bring glory to your name

Teach me your word Lord
Let it be my guiding light

Hold my hand Lord
You're the reason I can trust again

Lord, I surrender to You….Me

YOU ARE WORTHY

Written by Sharlette M. Franklin
6/6/87 Song of worship

VERSE 1
YOU ARE WORTHY, YOU ARE WORTHY
YOU ARE WORTH, LORD OF MY LIFE
YES, YOU ARE WORTHY

VERSE 2
YOU ARE HOLY, YOU ARE HOLY
YOU ARE HOLY, LORD OF MY LIFE
YES, YOU ARE HOLY

VERSE 3
YOU ARE WONDERFUL, YOU ARE WONDERFUL
YOU ARE WONDERFUL, LORD OF MY LIFE
YES, YOU ARE WONDERFUL

BRIDGE
AND I WILL PRAISE YOUR NAME
FOR EVERYDAY YOUR NAME IS THE SAME 2X

CAUSE YOU ARE WORTHY, LORD OF MY LIFE
YES, YOU ARE WORTHY

IN YOUR PRESENCE OH GOD

Written by Sharlette M. Franklin

11/23/04

IN YOUR PRESENCE OH GOD
I STAND NAKED BEFORE YOU
IN YOUR PRESENCE OH GOD
I HAVE NOTHING TO HIDE
IN YOUR PRESENCE OH GOD
I'M CONSUMED BY YOUR GLORY
IN YOUR PRESENCE
IN YOUR PRESENCE, OH GOD

CHORUS
IN YOUR PRESENCE
I FALL DOWN ON MY FACE
IN YOUR PRESENCE
I FEEL YOUR WARM EMBRACE
IN YOUR PRESENCE
VICTORY IS SET IN PLACE
AND FOR ME, IN YOUR PRESENCE
IS WHERE I WANT TO BE

BRIDGE
IT'S WHERE I WANT TO BE
IT'S WHERE I WANT TO BE
IN YOUR PRESENCE OH GOD
IS WHERE I WANT TO BE

Lord I Praise You

Written by Sharlette M. Franklin
9/3/04 in Clearwater Florida
In the midst of Hurricane Francis
God Reminded me that in the midst of the storm
My only job was to worship Him

Verse 1 (F, f/D, C, Bb, F/D, C/E, back to F)
Lord I praise You, Lord I praise You
Lord, I praise you, more than yesterday

Lord I praise you, Lord I praise you
Lord I praise you, more than anything

Chorus (C, Bb, C, F, C/E, Dm, C, Bb, C, C/E, F)
Stand by my side, never let me go
Hold me, mold me..
In you, there I'll hide

Verse 2
Lord I love you, Lord I love you
Lord I love you, more than yesterday

Lord I love you, Lord I love you
Lord I love you, more than anything

Chorus

HELP US HEAL

WRITTEN BY SHARLETTE M. FRANKLIN
9/15/01 IN HAWTHORNE, CA
THE AFTERMATH OF 9/11/01

VERSE 1

LORD WE REALLY NEED,
TO HEAR FROM YOU TODAY
WITH SO MANY OF OUR LOVED ONES
TAKEN AWAY, HEY

AND IN LIGHT OF MASS DESTRUCTION
WE AWAIT DIVINE INSTRUCTION
WE REPENT BEFORE YOU GOD
FOR OUR EVIL WAYS

HELP US AS WE HEAL
OUR WORLD TODAY

CHORUS

HELP US HEAL, HELP US NOW
DON'T DELAY, YOUR CONSUMING POWER (2x)

BRIDGE

FATHER WE NEED YOUR STRENGTH,
WE NEED YOUR LOVE
WE NEED YOUR FORGIVENESS IN OUR HEART

SO MASTER, TAKE US BY THE HAD
AS WE JOIN ACROSS THIS LAND
CAUSE WE NEED YOUR HEALING TODAY
FATHER WE NEED YOUR HEALING TODAY

Thank you again for allowing the blessings of God "shower" down on you as you go through your storm.

I solicit your prayers as I move forward and heed to the call of God on my life.

I too am taken to another level of faith as I obey God in the "things that I cannot see"

Hebrews 11:1

[1] Now faith is the substance of things hoped for, the evidence of things not seen

Author's Bio

Sharlette Marie Franklin is the author of Why Storms Are Needed along with several other inspirational and reference books. Also a songwriter, psalmist and prophet of the Most High God, Sharlette has ministered to thousands of people both in the U.S. and Europe. It is her desire to be able to circle the globe with the message of God's unconditional love and deliverance to those who will believe and receive Jesus the Christ.

Sharlette is the biological mother of two boys, who are the love of her life. She has a beautiful adopted daughter that constantly brings a smile to her face.

There are thousands more that call her their spiritual mother, from every walk of life and places around the world like Ireland, Cairo and Korea.

Since 1985, Sharlette has done the work of the ministry through allowing the love of God to be shown in her life towards everyone. Her mission and challenge is to enlighten, enhance and encourage the lives of people all over the world.

Her passion to change lives, heal wounded hearts and restore battered souls through love fulfills God's purpose.

She's willing to have a listening ear to many that call her for counseling on a daily basis. Sharlette loves to sing, pray and believe God for the miraculous for an individual that has almost given up hope.

When you encounter Sharlette, you immediately know that she comes to bring joy where there is sorrow and hope for someone's tomorrow.

It is a mission and a vision that will not die with Sharlette, but through her ministry of books, songs and powerful messages, her voice will continue for generations to come.

WHY STORMS ARE NEEDED

3 Stages of Faith

WRITTEN BY:

SHARLETTE M. FRANKLIN

ISBN: 978-0-6151-7669-7